The Music Scene

Music, Fashion and Style

Matt Anniss

W
FRANKLIN WATTS
LONDON • SYDNEY

This edition published in 2015 by
Franklin Watts
338 Euston Road
London NW1 3BH

Franklin Watts Australia
Level 17/207 Kent Street
Sydney, NSW 2000

© Franklin Watts 2015

Produced by Calcium, www.calciumcreative.co.uk

A CIP catalogue record for this book is available from
the British Library.

ISBN 978 1 4451 3940 1

Dewey classification: 338.4'778164

Printed in China

Franklin Watts is a division of Hachette Children's Books,
an Hachette UK company
www.hachette.co.uk

Acknowledgements:
The publisher would like to thank the following for permission to
reproduce photographs: Corbis: Condé Nast Archive 20bl, Henry
Diltz 19bl, Sunset Boulevard 13tr; Dreamstime: Daniel Garcia 6tr,
ImageCollect 14tr, Sean Pavone 32bl, Jose Antonio Sánchez Reyes 33tl,
Aaron Settipane 37tr; Getty Images: Redferns 24tr; Istockphoto: Izabela
Habur 15br; Library of Congress: United Press International 10; Rex
Features: Rick Colls 28bl, Everett Collection 8bl, Fraser Gray 23tr, Julian
Makey 31bl, Ilpo Musto 12bl, Armando Pietrangeli 9b, Suzy del Campo
/ PYMCA 31tr, Sipa Press 16bl, Ray Stevenson 21tr, Richard Young 40tr;
Shutterstock: Yuri Arcurs 23br, Chaoss 6bl, ChinellatoPhoto 42br, Dfree
34br, Elisanth cover, Featureflash 7br, 41cr, Adam Helweh 27br, iPhoto
Digital Events 5br, 38bl, Lemony 29tr, R. Gino Santa Maria 26tr, Nejron
Photo 35tr, Photobank.ch 22br, Photoproject.eu 17cr, Lev Radin 33br,
Joe Seer 19tr, Gordana Sermek 18cr, Nikola Spasenoski 36tr; Wikipedia:
Jose Garcia 25br, H. Grobe 11cr, Fabio Venni 30bl.

Every attempt has been made to clear copyright. Should there be any
inadvertent omission please apply to the publisher for rectification.

CONTENTS

CHAPTER ONE

FASHION AND POP

On street corners, teenage hip-hop fans hang out in their baggy jeans, trainers and baseball caps. Across town, a group of skate punks head down to a concert in skate shoes, band T-shirts and loose-fitting trousers. Elsewhere, dance music fans get ready for a rave.

The grunge style, originally made famous by Seattle bands in the early 1990s, continues to be popular 20 years on.

Dress to impress

For music fans around the world, clothes, hair and make-up choices are all influenced by the sounds that come out of their iPod earphones. Many music fans think following a band or a style of music is about belonging to a special group. Being a goth, punk, hip-hop head or heavy metal fan gives them a sense of identity. Like sports fans wearing the shirt of their favourite football or basketball team, they want people to know about their passion.

Goth style is as popular with today's teenagers as it was 30 years ago.

Distinctive clothes

There has always been more to the relationship between music and fashion than simply wanting to be part of a group. The musicians who set the trends have no need to fit in with a crowd. They wear the clothes that make them feel good, or help them to make an impression.

Love the style

Music, fashion and style are forms of creative expression. It's no coincidence that all three things are closely linked. After all, who hasn't watched a great music video and fallen in love not just with the song, but also the clothes the band are wearing?

Get the look

Top musicians want their own 'look'. To help them achieve this, they may work with leading fashion designers or stylists. The clothes they wear must be distinctive, but also appeal to would-be fans. If fans like what they see, they'll want to buy and wear the same clothes, or get the same haircut.

The goss

In March 2011, Britney Spears found herself in trouble following the launch of her fragrance, Radiance. Brand Sense said that she'd broken a contract with them to make the perfume. They sued, lost the case, appealed and eventually settled out of court in 2012.

Megabucks deals

Some music stars launch their own clothing ranges. Hip-hop billionaires such as Jay-Z, 50 Cent, and Sean 'Puffy' Combs have all supplemented their income from music by setting up their own fashion companies.

Coming up

In this book, we'll reveal how certain famous looks came about, how pop stars constantly change the way we all dress and why high street clothing stores look to music scenes for inspiration. We'll also explain how top musicians make millions of dollars through deals with clothing, perfume and make-up companies.

50 Cent makes millions of dollars every year from his G-Unit Clothing Company.

FASHION REVOLUTION

Music, fashion and style have not always been linked. During the first half of the twentieth century, there was little or no distinct 'pop culture'. All that changed in the 1950s thanks to a revolutionary form of music called rock and roll.

Not for parents

Musically, rock and roll didn't appeal to the older generation. Teenagers and young people liked it because it was loud, fun and great to dance to. Because their parents disliked the music, more and more young people started getting into rock and roll.

Role models

Rock and roll is important because it was about more than just music. Many rock and roll stars had their own distinct style that was soon copied by young people. Singers such as Gene Vincent and Elvis Presley wore tight jeans, white T-shirts and leather jackets. They slicked their hair back or sculpted it into quiffs using hair gel and wax such as Brylcreem.

Movie magic

The influence of rock and roll went further than the songs of Elvis or Buddy Holly. The look and attitude of rock-and-roll-loving teenagers quickly became a big part of popular Hollywood movies, too. Films such as *Rock Around the Clock*, *Jailhouse Rock* (starring Elvis Presley), *Don't Knock the Rock* and *Blue Denim* all featured teenage heroes who lived for music and fashion.

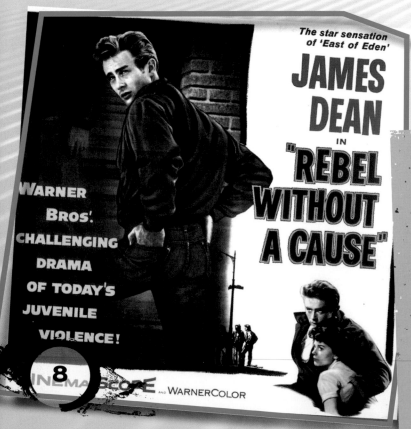

The star sensation of 'East of Eden'
JAMES DEAN IN "REBEL WITHOUT A CAUSE"
WARNER BROS'. CHALLENGING DRAMA OF TODAY'S JUVENILE VIOLENCE!
CINEMASCOPE AND WARNERCOLOR

Rebel role model

Perhaps the most influential movie of the era was 1955's *Rebel Without a Cause*, starring James Dean. In the film, he played a teenager who argued with his parents, dressed like a rock star and stood up to local bullies. The film was a runaway success. It made popular the idea of the teenager as a rebel who lived for rock and roll and dressed to impress.

Teddy Boys

In the UK, rock-and-roll-obsessed teens were called Teddy Boys. They dressed differently to US rockers. They liked to wear long drape jackets with a velvet trim, drainpipe trousers, white shirts, narrow ties and smart shoes such as brogues.

British Teddy Boys had a lot in common with US rock and roll fans, spending just as much time on their clothes and hair. Yet Teddy Boys took the rock and roll attitude to extremes. They hung around in gangs and sometimes caused trouble, fighting amongst themselves or with older people.

Teenage kicks

The fashion and style that formed around rock and roll music was a starting point for later teen music and fashion trends. Ever since, fans of both popular and less well-known musical styles have tried to stand out by dressing differently. Today's teenage music fans, whether they are hip-hop heads, goths or ravers, owe a lot to the rock and roll pioneers of the 1950s.

In the late 1950s, British Teddy Boys defined themselves by the clothes they wore and the rock and roll music they listened to.

THE BRITISH INFLUENCE

If the rock and roll revolution of the 1950s launched the concept of the teenager, the 1960s really cemented the relationship between young people, music and fashion.

High life

Many music fans couldn't afford the latest London fashions, but they could afford the clothes sold in department stores and high street shops. These clothes were inspired by the latest pop trends, such as mini-skirts and double-breasted suit jackets. High street fashion became a booming business worldwide, as more and more teenagers tried to look like their idols.

Surf's up

In the early 1960s, pop fashion moved away from the aggressive look of rockers, towards a more 'clean-cut' look. This was largely down to the success in the USA of Californian bands such as The Beach Boys, whose songs about surfing and open-top cars promoted a wholesome way of life. Their look of casual trousers, jackets and short-sleeved shirts reflected this ideal.

The British are coming

The clean-living image of The Beach Boys was a major influence on a band that became worldwide leaders in pop fashion – The Beatles. They'd grown up in Liverpool, UK, as leather-jacket-wearing rockers, but their manager Brian Epstein wanted them to replace their rough-edged style with a more wholesome look.

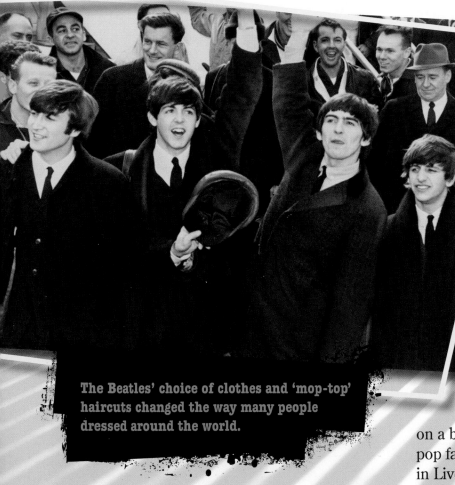

The Beatles' choice of clothes and 'mop-top' haircuts changed the way many people dressed around the world.

Beatlemania

Epstein decided that he wanted The Beatles to look smart, so he dressed them in collarless suits designed by the finest tailors in London. He added specially designed Beatle boots and mop-top haircuts. As The Beatles' fame spread, these trends became fashionable with young people all over the world.

Swinging London

The success of British bands in the USA helped to make London the most fashionable place on the planet. By the middle of the 1960s, mainstream fashions on both sides of the Atlantic were being set by the bands that shopped on the King's Road in Chelsea, or Carnaby Street in Soho.

In the 1960s, the King's Road in Chelsea, London, boasted some of the most fashionable clothes shops on the planet.

Vintage look

In recent years, the pop fashions of 1960s London have become popular again. This is down to the vintage revival seen in a number of modern pop stars. Perhaps the first of these to hit the headlines was singer Duffy, whose look and sound reaches back to the glory days of 1960s pop.

The goss

One of the most famous 'mod' bands of all time, The Who, wrote an album and film about the violent rivalry between mods and old-fashioned rockers in the 1960s. It was called Quadrophenia and told the story of one young mod's struggle against rockers and the establishment in the coastal town of Brighton, UK.

GLAMOUR BOYS AND GIRLS

Pop in the 1970s was a multi-coloured mix of sing-along rock and glamorous, disco-inspired dance music. As it had in the 1950s and '60s, fashion followed music. This time, it wasn't just teenage music fans dressing to impress, but people of all ages.

Glam jam

In the first half of the 1970s, it was the so-called 'glam rock' of acts such as David Bowie, T-Rex, Iggy Pop, Alice Cooper, and Lou Reed that caught the headlines. David Bowie set a trend by wearing platform boots with thick, ten-centimetre soles, all-in-one jumpsuits and glittery make-up.

Flare up

It was the boldness of the clothes that really caught on. Bell-bottomed flared trousers, wide ties and brightly coloured shirts were the clothes of choice for men in Western Europe and the USA.

The goss

London-based designer Mary Quant shaped the way women dressed in the 1970s. She first became famous in the 1960s for inventing the mini-skirt. She later found further fame by introducing the world to hot pants - tiny, tight shorts that became popular in the disco era.

With his love of outrageous clothes and ladies' make-up, singer David Bowie had a profound effect on the way men dressed in the 1970s.

Hot things

Women wore equally glamorous outfits, often featuring flared satin trousers, tight leather hot pants, mini-skirts and glitter-laden blouses or crop tops. In keeping with the musical fashion for glitter and eyeliner, women also wore super-bright make-up.

Tartan army

In the mid 1970s, one particular pop group set an unlikely trend for wearing tartan, a traditional Scottish fabric used for making kilts. The Bay City Rollers were a teen pop group from Edinburgh, Scotland, whose fame spread to the USA in 1976. As a sign of support, many of their teenage female fans would wear tartan scarves, traditional Scottish hats and even tight tartan trousers!

Disco fever

As the 1970s progressed, the pop charts became dominated by disco. This was a form of US dance music that began in New York City. Disco stars had their own unique dress sense, with men wearing a new version of the classic three-piece suit. To make the style more contemporary, designers added wide collars to shirts and flared bottoms to trousers.

Man-made style

Throughout the 1970s, music stars increased the popularity of clothes made from man-made fabrics such as polyester, nylon and Lycra. These clingy, often tight-fitting fabrics were revolutionary because they could be used to make clothes that had never been seen before.

Saturday night live

The classic 'disco look' was made popular by the film *Saturday Night Fever*, which featured John Travolta as a neighbourhood disco-dancing champion. Travolta's famous outfit became the blueprint for men's clothing the world over. Soon, everyone was wearing three-piece suits, tight flared trousers and brightly coloured polyester shirts.

13

TV FASHION

In the 1980s, the relationship between pop and fashion heated up. A new trend for music videos pushed the costumes and styles of music stars into the living rooms of millions of people around the world. Music Television, known as MTV, proved the turning point for many fashion trends.

Michael Jackson's music videos were hugely popular in the 1980s, leading many teenagers to copy his dance moves and bold choice of clothes.

Music makes fashion

MTV originally launched as a small-scale cable television channel in upstate New York in August 1981. It was the brainchild of a group of television executives who believed there was an appetite amongst young people for a 24-hour channel that showed nothing but music videos. They were quickly proved right. By the mid 1980s, MTV was cult viewing throughout the USA.

Video hits home

The success of MTV inspired many other television executives around the world to launch their own pop shows based on music videos. The music industry reacted to this boom by spending a lot more money on making music videos to promote their artists and their songs.

The Jackson effect

One artist who mastered the music video format was Michael Jackson. He hired leading 1980s movie director John Landis to make an extravagant video for the song *Thriller*. The Halloween-themed clip lasted 14 minutes and cost more than US$500,000 to make. It featured Jackson dancing with a troupe of zombies and was hugely successful.

Fashion icons

Michael Jackson wasn't the only 1980s pop star setting trends. Some teenagers wore ripped jeans, studded leather jackets and vests sported by big heavy metal and rock bands such as Poison and Aerosmith. Others dressed in designer Adidas or Nike shoes and casual sportswear like their hip-hop idols Run D.M.C. and The Beastie Boys.

Fad boys and sporty girls

There were many other fashion fads in the 1980s inspired by music videos. The leotard-and-leggings look in Olivia Newton-John's *Physical* single, the baggy parachute pants of MC Hammer and the frilly shirts and historical costumes worn by Adam and the Ants all set fashion trends. Thanks to these music videos and many, many others, fashion was a rapidly changing phenomenon in the 1980s.

The goss

Michael Jackson's *Thriller* was one of the most iconic music videos of the 1980s. It was more popular than many movies and was even shown in cinemas. Kids across the USA rushed to recreate Jackson's distinct look, which featured tight red leather trousers, a red and white leather jacket and a single white glove.

Use it up and wear it out

Thanks to the music video boom of the 1980s, teenagers could see exactly what their favourite pop stars were wearing. This meant that a pop star with their own distinct 'look' and an impressive video to match could quickly influence clothing trends. It also meant that fashions changed very quickly.

Pop music and fashion were closely linked in the 1980s. The popular 'Frankie Says Relax' T-shirts were inspired by a number one song by British band Frankie Goes to Hollywood.

Madonna

Few pop stars have set quite as many fashion trends as Madonna. Since first storming the international pop charts in 1983, Madonna has constantly remained one step ahead of her pop rivals. In the process, she's become one of the top fashion icons of the last 30 years.

Icon in waiting

Madonna has always been interested in fashion. In the late 1970s and early 1980s, she hung out at the most fashionable New York nightclubs. When she scored a contract with Sire Records in 1982, she quickly got together with New York designer Maripol to create a distinctive look that would get her noticed.

From the earliest days of her career, Madonna frequently changed her clothes and 'look' to reflect the latest cutting-edge fashion designs.

Pop rebel

With the assistance of Maripol, Madonna created a provocative look that combined bold, punk elements, religious icons such as crucifixes, and underwear worn over regular clothes. Madonna wore lace tops, fishnet stockings over Capri pants, and big jewellery.

Clothes horse

Madonna continued to change her clothes, style and appearance throughout the 1980s and 1990s. Her world tours offered a great opportunity to sport outrageous new costumes. In 1990, she asked leading French fashion designer Jean Paul Gaultier to design the outfits for her *Blond Ambition* tour. He created a number of designs that went on to become fashion classics.

Design for life

By the mid 1990s, Madonna was fully aware of her worth to fashion designers. Her videos and concerts were viewed by millions of people around the world. Many designers were keen to work with her.

Gaga inspiration

Madonna continues to reinvent her look, something that contemporary stars such as Lady Gaga have copied.

Madonna's look was unique and owed much to the New York club scene, but soon it would be the style of choice for teenage girls around the world. When she set out on her first world tour in 1985, she was amazed to see girls in the audience dressed like her. It was all down to her music videos, which were played endlessly on MTV.

Since the 1990s, Madonna has dressed as a cowgirl, worn clothes inspired by the Kabbalah religion and portrayed herself as a 1970s disco diva in hot pants and tight tops.

TIMELINE: Madonna

1983: Scores her first international hit with *Holiday*
1985: Tours the world, showcasing costumes designed by Maripol
1990: Works with French designer Jean Paul Gaultier for the first time
1993: *Blond Ambition* tour features clothes designed by Dolce & Gabbana
1997: Dresses as a cowgirl to promote her *Ray of Light* album
2006: Her *Confessions* tour features clothes from many top designers
2012: MDNA tour features clothes designed by top designers

CHAPTER TWO

PEACE, LOVE AND HATE

The relationship between music, fashion and style goes way beyond the designer brands and personal stylists of our top pop stars. Followers of underground and alternative music styles have always used clothes, hairstyles and make-up to help them stand out from the crowd.

Rebel wear

Dressing in a certain way shows others that you're a fan or follower of a certain type of music or cultural belief. This was certainly true of people who identified themselves as hippies in the late 1960s.

Hippy roots

The hippy movement began in the USA in the mid 1960s, when a writer called Ken Kesey and a group called The Merry Pranksters decided to travel around the country in a bus, spreading their message of peace, love and non-conformity. By 1967, their ideas had caught on in California, and specifically in a district of San Francisco known as Haight-Ashbury.

The hippy influence of the 1960s and 1970s can still be seen on fashion catwalks today.

Dropping out

At the height of the hippy movement, like-minded people from all over the USA would travel to Haight-Ashbury to 'turn on, tune in and drop out'. Hippies spent their time in local parks, playing and listening to music, enjoying the company of other hippies and protesting about US involvement in the Vietnam War.

Hippy days

Musical, cultural and artistic influences came together in the way hippies dressed. They wore loose shirts that featured handmade tie-dye patterns or Indian-style embroidery, headscarves and bell-bottomed trousers. Men and women both had their hair long and wore homemade jewellery.

Cultural movement

Many famous bands, including The Beatles, The Monkees and The Rolling Stones, started wearing 'hippy' style clothes and making music inspired by hippy culture.

Like many bands of the time, The Monkees fell in love with hippy style in the late 1960s.

The goss

The hippy look of the 1960s and '70s still influences the way people dress – particularly pop stars, models and actors. Since the mid 2000s, a look called 'Boho chic' has been made popular by stars and stylists, such as Rachel Zoe (above).

The Sex Pistols

Punk rock has its roots in New York in the early 1970s. Young bands such as The Ramones did not like the excesses of mainstream rock and pop. As a reaction to this, they created deliberately loud, simple and angry music – punk. By the end of the decade, punk had become more than just music for moody teenagers, it was a fashion movement as well.

Vivienne Westwood (right) leans against a telephone box with other punk girls on a London street in 1977.

The story begins

In 1975, punk rock musicians Steve Jones and Paul Cook went to a fashionable clothes shop on the King's Road in Chelsea, London, called Too fast to live, too young to die. The shop was run by Malcolm McLaren and his designer girlfriend, Vivienne Westwood.

Making history

Jones and Cook wanted to talk to McLaren about managing their band, The Strand. The businessman had been to New York and was inspired by the outrageous look of The Ramones and New York Dolls. Jones and Cook thought McLaren could help them hit the big time.

Rough cut

McLaren and Westwood spotted an opportunity. Westwood had started designing clothes inspired by the US punk rock movement. If McLaren managed Cook and Jones' band, Westwood could dress them in her new punk fashion designs. It was a great plan and the outrageous group (renamed The Sex Pistols by McLaren) very quickly became the most famous UK band by far of 1976.

The punk look

At the time, most bands wore bold and garish clothes inspired by disco, such as jumpsuits and glittery shirts. Westwood kitted The Sex Pistols out in ripped jeans, leather jackets held together by safety pins and T-shirts featuring provocative slogans. They were encouraged to act as controversially as possible.

Fashion movement

By the summer of 1977, punk music and fashion had become an obsession with British and US teenagers. Westwood's clothes proved

The Sex Pistols' torn clothes and rowdy live shows inspired a whole new music and fashion movement: punk.

the inspiration for a whole new punk look. Young men and women made their own punk outfits using safety pins, lavatory chains, studded leather jackets and ripped T-shirts.

The end of the Pistols

The Sex Pistols released their debut album in 1977, but split up in 1978 at the end of their first sell-out tour of the USA. By then, punk rock and fashion were firmly established in the hearts of teenagers across the world.

TIMELINE: Punk

1975: Businessman Malcolm McLaren visits New York and is excited by the new punk fashions of The Ramones

1976: The Sex Pistols form and are dressed by fashion designer Vivienne Westwood

1994: Green Day make pop-punk fashionable worldwide

2000: Pop-punk continues its rise thanks to the success of The Offspring and Blink-182

2002: Footballer David Beckham wears a punk-inspired Mohawk haircut

TWO TRIBES

The early 1980s were an exciting time for underground music, with new sounds and styles appearing all the time. Each new sound had its own look, which was seen by teenagers in the music videos shown on MTV.

Darkness and misery

One of the most popular underground music styles at the time was goth (short for 'gothic'). This brand of indie-rock appealed to teenagers in the USA and UK due to its dark, moody sounds and miserable lyrics. Leading goth bands such as The Cult, Joy Division, Sisters of Mercy and The Cure often wore jet-black clothes and dark make-up, dying their hair black to complete the striking look.

Don't stop the goth

Fans of gothic rock often wore similar clothes to identify themselves with the musical movement. The typical goth look was inspired by a mix of different historical influences. Both men and women wore dark eyeliner and black lipstick. The goth look influenced the early style of singer Madonna.

The classic gothic look was inspired by a mix of horror films, dark 1980s pop music and clothes from the 1900s.

Future heads

Another popular music-inspired youth movement was 'futurism'. The 1980s 'futurists' were fans of cutting-edge electronic music and synthesiser pop. Following bands such as Duran Duran, Depeche Mode, The Human League, Heaven 17 and Cabaret Voltaire, young futurists wore eyeliner, long trench coats, leather trousers and baggy white shirts. Some futurists also wore blue RAF jackets and lanyards (ropes) instead of jewellery.

New rock

Futurism wasn't quite as popular in the USA. Many US teenagers weren't interested in music made using synthesisers and preferred a loud new style of rock – heavy metal. Heavy metal and heavy rock bands were deliberately outrageous. They made very loud music and lived wild lifestyles. They had no time for making themselves look good and instead wore ripped jeans, denim jackets, long hair and sleeveless T-shirts or vests. Bands such as Van Halen, Kiss, Aerosmith, Iron Maiden, Judas Priest and Def Leppard became huge stars. It wasn't long before US teenagers were copying their style.

Get the look

Not all US teenagers were fans of heavy rock and heavy metal. Some wore casual sportswear like their hip-hop idols, others T-shirts with slogans. Many opted for the T-shirt/jacket combination worn by white 'Blue-eyed soul' acts such as Hall and Oates, while others styled their hair in the jheri curl style worn by funk singers such as Prince.

The goss

One musician did much to popularise the 'futurist' look. Phil Oakey was the lead singer of a new wave synth-pop band called The Human League. His distinctive haircut featured a long fringe combed to the right and was copied by lots of his fans.

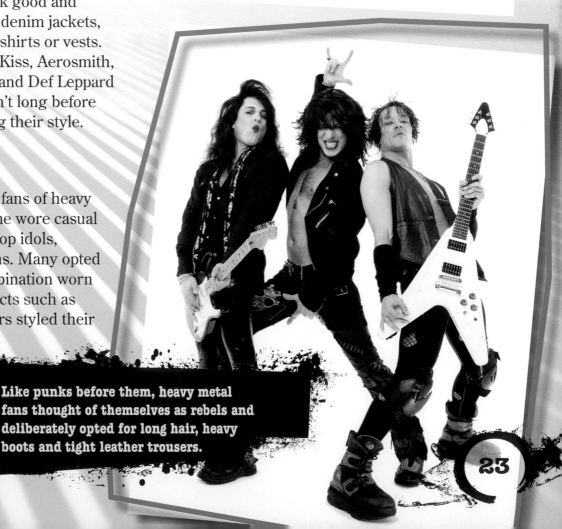

Like punks before them, heavy metal fans thought of themselves as rebels and deliberately opted for long hair, heavy boots and tight leather trousers.

23

ROUGH TRADE

In the early 1990s, a form of indie-rock music called grunge took the world by storm. In the process, its casually-dressed stars set a new fashion trend for dressing down, not dressing up.

The Seattle sound

The roots of grunge lie in the US city of Seattle in the mid to late 1980s. There, a number of energetic but deliberately under-produced rock bands recorded a whole new style of music for a small record label called Sub Pop. Groups such as Sonic Youth, Soundgarden and Pearl Jam excited music fans with the rawness of their music, which was at odds with the glossy mainstream rock sound of the time.

Smells Like Teen Spirit

The band that helped launch grunge to a wider audience was Nirvana. Led by their charismatic frontman Kurt Cobain, who later tragically killed himself, Nirvana wowed listeners with their brilliant 1991 album *Nevermind*. The album contained a song that would become an anthem for a generation of music lovers – *Smells Like Teen Spirit*.

Early grunge acts such as Sonic Youth (pictured) found their clothes in thrift stores and charity shops.

Anti-fashion

Like other grunge bands of the period, Nirvana weren't particularly bothered about fashion. On stage and in their popular music videos, they wore second-hand clothes found in thrift stores or charity shops, faded T-shirts and stained denim jeans. They rarely bothered combing their hair, instead leaving it unwashed and unruly. The grunge look was not so much fashionable as 'anti-fashion'.

New trend

The casual, almost dishevelled look seen in grunge bands would go on to set a trend for indie-rock music. It became fashionable to dress in old, tattered or well-worn clothes. Soon, MTV was full of videos featuring scruffy indie-rock and grunge bands. Mainstream fashion designers began to take note.

Fashion fix

The fashion industry responded to the grunge movement by creating new clothes with a grunge look. They also used some of the scene's biggest stars to sell their wares.

Geek chic

British indie-rock bands quickly followed the trend set by their US peers. Early 1990s 'shoegazing' bands wore baggy, long-sleeved T-shirts along with jeans and Doc Marten boots. Later 1990s bands such as Pulp dressed primarily in geek chic outfits featuring faded 1970s clothing rescued from charity shops.

Lasting legacy

The casual grunge look set a trend in indie-rock music that still exists to this day. Since grunge hit the mainstream, most indie-rock bands and fans dress casually in jeans, T-shirts and battered old trainers or Doc Marten boots.

The goss

When asked to explain the popularity of the grunge look in a magazine interview, Sub Pop Records boss Jonathan Poneman said: 'The clothing is cheap, durable and timeless. It also runs against the grain of the whole flashy aesthetic that existed in the 1980s.'

The casual grunge look lives on in the outfits sported by stars such as Avril Lavigne.

BEAT THE STREET

One of the biggest shifts in fashion over the last three decades has been the growth of streetwear. This is fashion inspired by the casual but often stylish day-to-day outfits of young people. In many cases, the origins of these outfits can be traced back to music scenes, stars or videos. This is certainly the case with the original streetwear phenomenon – hip-hop.

Get sporty

Back in the early 1980s, when rap music and hip-hop culture were first emerging, the idea of wearing sportswear as a fashion choice was exciting. Before this, the only people who wore sportswear were athletes.

Ruthless rap assassins

In the mid 1980s, the world was beginning to wake up to a form of music that had emerged from the tough streets of New York City in the late 1970s. Hip-hop was performed by 'rappers' who wore tracksuits, baseball caps and chunky gold jewellery. It was like nothing that had ever gone before.

Casual appeal

To 1980s teenagers, especially those outside of New York, part of the appeal of hip-hop and rap music was the exciting look of the scene's new stars. To kids who'd grown up watching pop stars in designer outfits or outrageous clothes, the casual but bold look of rappers was an amazing development. It wasn't long before hip-hop fans began to copy the clothes worn by Run D.M.C., Kurtis Blow, and The Beastie Boys.

Hip-hop style

The 1980s hip-hop look was striking on one hand, and impressively casual on the other. Typical outfits would feature tracksuits, gold chains, T-shirts and baseball caps, or baggy trousers (sometimes jeans), smart hats and bomber jackets. Most rappers wore very expensive trainers.

The trainer

Throughout the 1980s, the most important items in any hip-hop fan's wardrobe were their trainers. Trainers were more important than the rest of their outfit put together.

Marketing magic

Major sportswear manufacturers soon realised the potential in marketing their clothes and trainers to the hip-hop community. It was a smart move. As the popularity of hip-hop spread around the world, so did the popularity of their premium sportswear.

The goss

The 1980s rap heavyweights Run D.M.C. summed up hip-hop's obsession with fashionable trainers on their 1986 single My Adidas. The track helped secure them a US$1.6 million endorsement deal with the German sportswear giant – the first in the history of hip-hop.

Bling beginnings

As hip-hop changed and became more popular in the 1990s and 2000s, so did the way its biggest stars dressed. It became more about wearing the hottest high-end brands, from Tommy Hilfiger to Versace and Rolex.

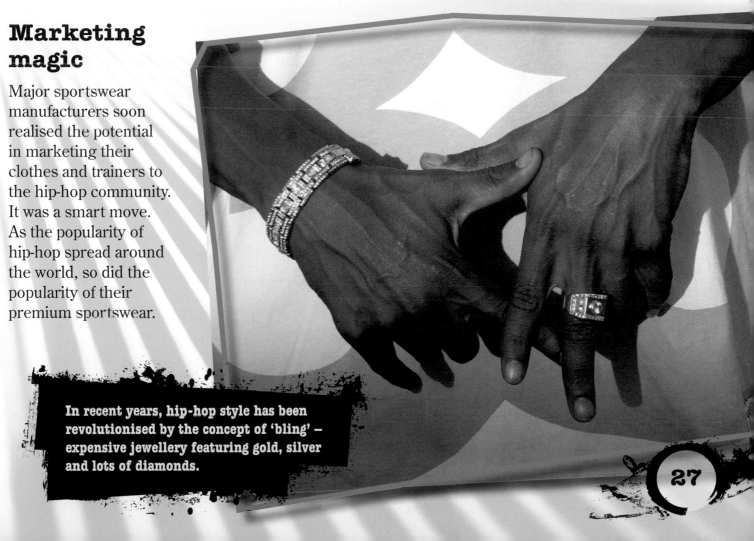

In recent years, hip-hop style has been revolutionised by the concept of 'bling' – expensive jewellery featuring gold, silver and lots of diamonds.

27

THIS IS ACID

The growth of streetwear in the 1980s and 1990s had an influence on more than just the day-to-day clothing of young people. It also changed the way people dressed to go out to dance, as a huge explosion in the popularity of dance music took hold on both sides of the Atlantic.

Tried and tested

Traditionally, going out to dance clubs was the highlight of many people's week. Men and women went out to dance to the latest pop, soul, funk or disco tunes in mainstream clubs.

Going underground

Even at underground nightclubs, where young people would go and dance to alternative music styles, a focus on fashion was encouraged. In some cases, this would mean dressing in the style of the music being played – futurism, goth or new romantic.

This is acid

The arrival of a new form of music called acid house changed everything. In 1988, the UK and the USA experienced what became the second 'summer of love'. Hundreds of thousands of teenagers gathered in fields at illegal raves to dance to the latest acid house music to hit the dance scene.

The early 1990s rave scene was founded on the principle of 'being yourself'. This meant that dancers could wear whatever they liked, as long as it was comfortable.

Love and happiness

Acid house had a profound effect on young people. Before house, music fans were often very tribal and stuck to clubs that played music they knew and liked. Acid house brought fans of many different music styles together. They just wanted to dance and have a good time.

Boom times

On the back of the second summer of love, rock musicians began incorporating elements of dance music into their songs. Attitudes to fashion changed.

One love

Acid house broke down barriers in the way people dressed when they went out. Instead of wearing the tribal uniforms that identified them as fans of a certain style, teenagers began wearing more ordinary, casual clothes which were comfortable to dance in.

The goss

The single most popular item amongst ravers in the late 1980s was the acid house smiley T-shirt. This featured a big, round, yellow smiley face. The logo became popular after it was used in the video to Bomb the Bass's top ten single *Beat Dis*.

Be yourself

Club fashion has changed since the 1980s, but the commitment to dress comfortably and 'be yourself' has remained. If you visited an underground nightclub today, you would find some people dressed in the latest fashions, some more casually and others in urban designs influenced by hip-hop.

Smiley culture

Trainers, baggy jeans and long-sleeved T-shirts became popular with ravers. Some revisited the loose, late 1960s look of US hippies, while others found influence in contemporary fashion, following magazines such as *The Face*.

TUNING IN

For many years, high street fashion has followed youth music trends. This has never been more apparent than in recent years. Street-savvy teenagers and young people tune in to music that takes the best of the past and present and offers something new and fresh.

Indie-dance returns

There has traditionally been little crossover between indie-rock and dance, both musically and in fashion. Yet in the mid 2000s, a new wave of indie-dance bands began to emerge. These new groups took the best of both styles and created something completely new.

Nu-rave wave

Fashion quickly followed suit, responding to these new sounds with a distinctive look that was coined nu-rave. It paired the tight-fitting, low-slung skinny jeans seen on indie-rockers with the off-the-shoulder girls' tops and baggy T-shirts once worn by 1980s ravers.

For a brief period, nu-rave was massive. Teenagers bought music downloads by bands such as the Klaxons and Simian Mobile Disco and dressed in typical nu-rave outfits.

Dance act Simian Mobile Disco were at the forefront of a new movement in music and fashion called nu-rave.

The goss

The most influential nu-rave scene in the world was based in Paris and centred on a record label called Ed Banger. The label's artists created their own look, using traditional rock items such as leather trousers and jackets with vintage T-shirts, white-rimmed sunglasses and 1980s-inspired haircuts.

Making a comeback

On the back of nu-rave, many bands started to gain inspiration from synthesiser sounds of the 1980s. Fashion stores once again followed suit, offering young people the chance to buy designs influenced by major 1980s clothing trends. Leggings, Lycra 'pop tops' and Capri pants all made a comeback, alongside clothes in bright neon colours.

Vintage revival

This desire to look back for inspiration, both musically and in the way people dress, has continued to this day. Vintage clothing has become increasingly popular, from 1940s and 1950s inspired dresses, shirts and blouses to tight-fitting T-shirts featuring 1970s and '80s designs.

All change

In an age where musical trends quickly change thanks to online access to tracks, so too does fashion. By the time you read this, a whole new musical movement will have emerged and the way young people dress will have shifted to reflect that.

The distinctive nu-rave look was inspired by a mix of early '90s rave clothing, 1980s style and hip-hop sportswear.

Urban warriors

Recent urban fashion items include big earrings inspired by African culture, baseball caps and Burberry-check caps (left). T-shirts featuring 1980s style slogans or hand-drawn illustrations, shorts and baggy or skinny jeans have also made a comeback.

BIG IN JAPAN

It's easy to think of the USA and UK as the driving force behind pop fashion. Yet over the last two decades, one nation has embraced streetwear more than any other – Japan.

Changing times

Traditionally, Japanese people have been quite conservative in the way they dress and act. Yet, as the country has become richer and more successful over the last 50 years, attitudes have completely changed.

Money to burn

Young people in Japan have more spare money to spend than their counterparts in Europe and the USA. Because of this, more CDs and music downloads are sold in Japan than in any other country except the USA. Streetwear inspired by US and European pop fashion is hugely popular with the nation's young people.

Individual style

Japanese teenagers like to dress to impress. Instead of sticking to one style, many young people will create their own outfits by mixing clothes and hairstyles made popular by Western and Japanese (J-pop) musicians.

Cutting-edge

The outfits created by young people in Japan are often far bolder and more outrageous than those worn by teenagers in the USA. High street stores in Japan sell clothes many in the West would consider to be cutting-edge.

Fashion fusion

One famous example of Japanese street fashion at its most outrageous and distinct is the Lolita look.

The goss

The Harajuku district of Tokyo is widely considered to be the streetwear capital of the world. It features many small fashion boutiques and shops selling cutting-edge clothing designs. Every Sunday, teenagers gather in Harajuku in their best outfits to hang out with their friends.

Worldwide success

Japanese fashion is now incredibly popular worldwide. In a neat twist, many top US rap stars now wear clothes made in Japan, such as Evisu jeans. The brand has been mentioned in tracks by Jay-Z, Young Jeezy, and Lil' Wayne. The Neptunes star Pharrell Williams is such a fan of Japanese clothing that he invested in A Bathing Ape, one of Japan's leading brands. Even singer Gwen Stefani launched her own Japanese-inspired range of clothes, Harajuku Lovers, in 2005.

The popular Japanese Lolita punk style has an edgy but cute look.

Originally inspired by the dresses, corsets and suits worn by Europeans in the nineteenth century, it has taken on many influences from twentieth-century musical styles. Examples include Lolita goth and punk.

After visiting Tokyo while on tour, Gwen Stefani launched her own range of clothes inspired by Japanese style and culture.

Rap attack

Hip-hop is particularly big in Japan. Since first taking hold amongst Tokyo's teenagers in the early 1990s, it has helped to shape the way many young Japanese dress. Some Japanese hip-hop fans go even further than dressing like their rap idols, choosing to darken their faces with make-up to look more like black Americans.

WEB STYLE

Over the last 15 years, the Internet has changed the way people communicate, shop and use their leisure time. It has also had an incredible effect on the music and fashion industries.

The dark ages

Before the Internet, music fans got their information about new bands or forthcoming releases from television, radio, newspapers and magazines. Because of this, music and fashion trends changed relatively slowly, usually following recommendations from a handful of journalists around the world.

Everything changes

The explosion of music and fashion blogs in the late 2000s changed everything. Amateurs and would-be journalists decided to share their thoughts with the

world. In music, bloggers championed new music styles and unheard bands, while the fashion world was turned upside down by bloggers championing little-known designers or their own ideas on bold new outfits.

Get with the band

Many musicians and bands have capitalised on this music and fashion revolution by selling their own T-shirts and fashion items directly to fans online. Others collaborate with their favourite designers to launch limited edition items that are only available at concerts. More than ever, music fashion is in the hands of musicians and fans rather than traditional designers.

When stars such as Katy Perry blog a photograph of themselves wearing a different hair colour, it can start a new trend overnight.

She's in fashion

In the early days, many fashion blogs were focused on high-end fashion and famous brands. One of the first early fashion bloggers to find success was Kathryn Finney of *The Budget Fashionista*. Her blog was so influential, she was invited to attend New York Fashion Week in 2003.

People power

In recent years, there has been a huge increase in blogs focusing on street fashion – fashion trends that emerge from underground music scenes, developed by real people rather than fashion designers.

Changing the fashion world

Music and fashion blogs are particularly important to both industries because they influence major trends. Blogs can be updated quickly, helping fashion-conscious teenagers to find the latest looks or sounds quicker than ever before.

Internet fashion bloggers have replaced fashion journalists as the taste-makers of the twenty-first century.

The goss

In 2007, journalist Robin Givhan used an article in fashion magazine Harper's Bazaar to claim that blogs had changed the fashion business. He said: 'The average person, too often estranged from fashion, is taking ownership of it.'

Blog on

In recent years, the effect of fashion and music blogs on both industries has been vast. For example, many young, unknown T-shirt designers have created popular designs based on music icons, trends or slogans. These sell in large amounts thanks to blog postings. The '80s revival (in music and fashion) and the rise in urban dance culture also have the support of blogs to thank for their popularity.

CHAPTER FOUR

BIG BUSINESS

In the twenty-first century, the lines between music, fashion, style and business have become increasingly blurred. Many top recording artists now sign multimillion dollar deals with clothing or cosmetics brands, while others set up their own fashion companies.

Brand ambassadors

Clothing brands and manufacturers of high-end fashion accessories such as perfumes have seen the potential of music stars as 'brand ambassadors'. Signing-up a star can be a quick, if expensive, way of getting great publicity and increasing awareness of a product. In most cases, the endorsement of a top musician can boost sales significantly.

Wealth talks

In the late twentieth- and early twenty-first century, no one area of music has been more heavily involved in brand endorsement than hip-hop and R&B. In the 1990s, the scene's top stars such as Jay-Z and Sean Paul used their records to rap about money and wealth. The obsession with money, wealth and material possessions was known as 'bling bling'.

Missy Elliott struck a multimillion dollar endorsement deal with German sportswear giant Adidas and has even designed clothes for the company.

Top stars would regularly wear expensive watches and oversized jewellery. They would also rap about other products associated with great wealth, such as champagne and the latest fashionable clothes.

Endorsements

Given their status as huge global stars, it wasn't long before big companies started approaching musicians to endorse their products. Missy Elliott landed a deal to promote her own clothing range with sportswear brand Adidas, while Beyoncé launched her own brand of perfume with Tommy Hilfiger, called True Star.

The goss

One of the R&B artists who has profited most from product endorsement is Rihanna. In the last decade, she has had endorsement deals with cosmetics brands Nivea and Clinique, sportswear brand Nike and top fashion house Gucci.

Fashion future

Some global hip-hop stars are not happy endorsing other people's products and have moved into fashion themselves. A number of top rappers now own huge clothing and fashion companies. They use their star status to help promote their ranges.

Fashion billionaires

Many big hip-hop stars now have business interests in the fashion world. N.E.R.D. singer Pharrell Williams owns a clothing company called Billionaire Boys Club, which he founded with Japanese fashion designer Nigo. Jay-Z was also part-owner of urban fashion brand Rocawear until recently. His wife Beyoncé owns a clothing company called House of Dereon and 50 Cent has a multimillion dollar deal with Reebok.

P. Diddy

One of the most successful rappers-turned-businessmen is Sean Combs. He launched his line of fashionable men's clothes, Sean John, in 1998. Since then, it has grown to be one of the most popular lines in the USA, winning fashion design awards. In 2008, he added to his fashion interests by buying the Encye clothing brand.

Grace Jones

Many musicians still prefer to dress in clothes created by top fashion designers. The relationship between underground music and high-end fashion goes back a long way. Since the 1970s, one artist has covered all three like no other – Grace Jones.

Striking model

Born in the Caribbean, Grace Jones first made a name for herself as a catwalk model in New York, Paris, London and Milan in the mid 1970s. As a tall black woman with striking looks and a passion for haircuts usually worn by men, she was one of the most distinctive and in-demand models of her time.

Having started her career as a catwalk model for top fashion designers, singer Grace Jones knows more than most pop stars about cutting-edge clothes and outrageous costumes.

38

Pop art

While in New York, Jones hooked up with famous artist Andy Warhol, who made his name in the 1950s and 1960s by leading the pop art movement. He photographed the young model and took her to Studio 54, the most famous club of the era.

New York icon

Because of her looks, famous modelling career and love of disco music, Jones quickly became an icon in New York's gay scene. It wasn't long before Island Records offered her a recording contract.

Grace's portfolio

Jones released her first album, a collection of disco tracks called *Portfolio*, in 1977. Although it wasn't a huge success, Jones recorded two more albums of disco before switching her attention to reggae and new wave pop. Because of Jones' modelling career, her records received plenty of press coverage.

Rhythm queen

In 1985, Jones released her most widely acclaimed project, a concept album called *Slave to the Rhythm*. Unlike regular albums,

Bond girl

Grace Jones' most famous film role was as unlikely Bond girl May Day in the 1985 James Bond movie *A View to a Kill*. She starred alongside Roger Moore and the film's villain, Christopher Walken.

it didn't feature a set of songs but rather various interpretations of the title track. It was adventurous and lived up to her reputation as someone at the cutting-edge of fashion and music.

She's a model

Slave to the Rhythm contained a number of references to Jones' modelling career. One of the tracks was called *The Fashion Show*, while others featured interviews with the singer.

Groundbreaking

Slave to the Rhythm was one of the most significant records of the 1980s. It perfectly summed up the working relationship between underground club culture, cutting-edge electronic music and high fashion.

TIMELINE: Grace Jones

1975: Begins modelling career, sharing a Paris apartment with Jerry Hall
1977: Lands record deal with Island Records
1981: Releases *Pull Up to the Bumper*, her biggest club hit
1985: Stars as May Day in the James Bond movie *A View to a Kill*
2006: Appears as a catwalk model again for Diesel at the brand's New York show
2013: Named as one of the fifty best-dressed women over 50 by the *Guardian* newspaper

39

THE BRIT SCENE

In the 1960s, a rise in popularity of British music around the world, and particularly in the USA, led to a renewed focus on the country's fashion scene. Britain's fashion, style and cosmetics industries received a similar boost in the 1990s and early 2000s thanks to a new boom time for British music.

Dual inspirations

There were two inspirations for this British revival. First, there was Britpop, a form of indie-rock music that borrowed heavily from the sounds of 1960s swinging London. Then there was The Spice Girls (a pop band aimed at teenage girls), who became superstars around the world.

God save the Queen

Both The Spice Girls and Britpop heroes such as Oasis and Blur were proud of their British roots. Oasis songwriter Noel Gallagher often appeared on stage with a guitar featuring the country's Union Jack flag, while Blur's songs focused on life in London.

Spice World

The Spice Girls showed their support for British culture by wearing clothes such as Union Jack dresses.

When Spice Girls' singer Geri Halliwell appeared at the Brit Awards wearing a Union Jack dress, it launched a whole new craze for British fashion designs.

They starred in their own movie, *Spice World*, which featured a London double-decker bus painted in red, white and blue.

Cool Britannia

The Spice Girls and Oasis had great success in the USA. Their brands of British pop were a hit with teenagers and 20-something music buyers. It wasn't long before US magazines such as *Rolling Stone* and *Newsweek* were saying that London was 'swinging' again. The British revival was dubbed Cool Britannia – a pun on the patriotic British song *Rule Britannia*.

The goss

The term 'Cool Britannia' was first used in the 1960s, but became popular in the 1990s thanks to ice cream makers Ben & Jerry's. They trademarked the term to refer to a limited edition flavour of their ice cream containing British staples such as strawberries, cream and shortbread biscuit pieces.

Fashion boom

Cool Britannia was about more than music. With London once again the centre of attention, the British fashion industry enjoyed a new period of global dominance. British models Kate Moss and Naomi Campbell became the poster girls for clothes by British fashion designers Alexander McQueen and Stella McCartney.

Swinging London town

In 1997, leading fashion magazine *Vanity Fair* published a special issue under the headline 'London Swings Again'. It featured Oasis singer Liam Gallagher and actress Patsy Kensit on the cover, plus interviews with Alexander McQueen and Blur guitarist Graham Coxon.

The face of London

Model Kate Moss was one of the key figures in Cool Britannia. She not only modelled the latest British fashions, but also hung out with top pop stars in London. She quickly became the face of the Rimmel make-up brand, which relaunched as Rimmel London to cash in on the US passion for British products.

Model Kate Moss was a central figure in what the press called 'Cool Britannia' – an upsurge in the popularity of British clothes and music in the late 1990s.

Lady Gaga

Madonna built a long music career by wearing outrageous costumes and by having a close relationship with top fashion designers. Today, there is a new queen of pop fashion – Lady Gaga.

Global icon

Lady Gaga has sold millions of CDs worldwide. Her single *Poker Face* is reportedly the most downloaded song of all time. Yet like Madonna before her, Lady Gaga has built her reputation on more than just music. First entering the pop charts in 2007, she is known just as much for her cutting-edge clothes and bold make-up as her catchy songs.

Dressed for success

During her time as a burlesque performer, Lady Gaga began to play around with her on-stage look. She created outfits that mixed

Like Madonna before her, Lady Gaga is as famous for her outrageous clothes and costumes as her top-selling pop hits.

the glam rock style of David Bowie, disco glamour, Madonna's revolutionary early 1980s look and contemporary catwalk fashions.

Over the top

But Lady Gaga didn't stop there. She added influences from the burlesque scene, such as intense make-up and over-the-top hairstyles. By the time she became a global star in the late 2000s, she'd created a daring and outrageous look all of her own.

Talking point

Since making it big, Lady Gaga has received just as much coverage in fashion magazines as she has in music magazines. For every new live show she introduces a string of new outfits. She works with a variety of well-known and up-and-coming fashion designers in order to stay ahead of her rivals.

Award winner

In 2010, Lady Gaga was listed as one of *British Vogue's* '10 Best Dressed People' of the year, while her stylist Nicola Formichetti was named Fashion Creator of the Year at the 2010 British Fashion Awards. Lady Gaga also writes a column for US fashion magazine *V*, about the design of her unique outfits.

Underground beginnings

Before she became a big star, Lady Gaga spent time in various underground bands, playing strange electronic and alternative rock music. Unable to secure a record contract, she quit and began singing and dancing in underground New York clubs, and specifically the controversial burlesque scene.

Lasting influence

Although operating at the more cutting-edge end of fashion, Lady Gaga has had a huge effect on high street fashion in Europe and the USA. Her passion for outrageous outfits has caught on with mainstream designers and young women in general. In just the short time in which she has risen to fame, she has become an iconic figure in pop fashion.

TIMELINE: Lady Gaga

2005: Records her first professional song with rap legend Grandmaster Melle Mel

2006: Adopts Lady Gaga name and works as a burlesque performer

2007: Signs to Interscope Records

2008: Debut single *Just Dance* rockets to the top of the US charts

2010: Causes controversy by wearing a dress made from meat

2014: Releases jazz album, *Cheek to Cheek*, with Tony Bennett

GLOSSARY

aesthetic how something looks

alternative different

amateurs enthusiastic people who do something as an unpaid hobby

blueprint a detailed plan

boutiques small, independently-run shops

burlesque a style of entertainment featuring songs, dancing and comedy routines that became popular in the nineteenth century

Capri pants a style of trousers that are noticeably shorter than regular trousers, often worn by women

championing campaigning for or enthusiastically talking about something

charismatic someone who is persuasive and charming

conservative to be traditional or cautious of change

controversial something that upsets some people and delights others

creative expression anything that allows someone to be creative, for example designing clothes or making music

crossover the point where two or more music or fashion styles come together to form something new

crucifixes the Christian cross, usually displayed outside a church. Smaller versions are often worn as jewellery

cult viewing a term used to refer to television programmes, shows or films watched by large groups of people, but not necessarily popular with the public at large

diva a celebrated female singer

double-breasted a coat or suit jacket featuring two parallel rows of buttons and overlapping flaps

drainpipe tight-fitting jeans or trousers

electronic music music made using computers and electronic instruments such as keyboards and drum machines

endorsement deal an agreement in which a star wears a company's clothing or shoes in exchange for payment

establishment a term used to refer to people in positions of power, for example politicians, policemen and business people

estranged separated

executives the people at the top of a big company, such as a record label

fashion house a fashion industry term for a company that makes fashionable clothing

fishnet stockings stockings featuring a diamond stitch pattern

grunge a popular style of 1990s US rock music, so-called because of the casual, often unwashed clothes worn by bands

iconic famous and memorable

identity what makes people different, such as their clothes, personality or taste in music

illegal raves big, unlicensed dance music events held outdoors

indie-rock alternative rock music – 'indie' is short for 'independent'

influential someone or something that helps to change the way people think or act

jheri curl a 1980s hairstyle featuring loose curls, popular amongst black musicians

Kabbalah religion a traditional religion based on Judaism (a Jewish religion)

kilts a traditional Scottish item of clothing for men and women, which looks like a skirt

mainstream popular and well-known

Mohawk haircut when the head is shaved except for a band down the scalp's middle

mop-top a popular 1960s haircut inspired by The Beatles

neon a gas used to make flashing signs. Also very bright colours that don't look natural

nu-rave a mid 2000s music and fashion movement inspired by clothes, make-up and dance music of the early 1990s

patriotic to be proud of your nationality

personal stylists people who assist stars with their make-up and clothes

phenomenon a massive or unusual event

pioneers people who do something first, before anyone else

polyester a man-made fabric

pop culture a collective term for music, art, books, fashion, films and television

potential capable of becoming something, for example a big star or famous musician

premium expensive or top of the range

promote to encourage the sales of something by publicising it, for example through advertisements or media interviews

provocative designed to get an extreme reaction from viewers or listeners

R&B a popular style of soul music – short for 'rhythm and blues'

reinvent to come up with a whole new style, sound or personality from scratch

revival to bring something back, for example old music or clothes

rivalry heated competition between two or more people, or groups of people

shoegazing a style of British rock music popular in the early 1990s, so-called because some musicians stared at their feet, rather than looking at the audience

slogans phrases or mottos used to sell products

synthesiser pop a style of popular music largely made using synthesiser keyboards

tailors people who make clothes for a living

timeless something that lasts the test of time, such as a style of clothing or piece of music

trademarked something protected by a 'trademark' (a binding legal document)

tribal a term used to refer to how people behave in groups, for example those who like a style of music or clothing

under-produced music designed to sound raw, unpolished or unfinished

underground alternative or less popular

Vietnam War a war in Vietnam, Asia, between 1955 and 1975, in which 58,000 US soldiers and over 2 million Vietnamese died

FURTHER READING

Books

The Teen Vogue Handbook: An Insider's Guide to Careers in Fashion (Puffin, 2010)

Bonnie English: *Fashion – The 50 Most Influential Fashion Designers of All Time* (Barron's Educational Series, 2010)

Bonnie English: *A Cultural History of Fashion in the 20th Century – From the Catwalk to the Sidewalk* (Berg Publishers, 2007)

Richard Martin, Alice Mackrell, Melanie Rickey, Angela Buttolph, Suzy Menkes: *The Fashion Book* (Phaidon Press, 2001)

Websites

Find out more about streetwear from around the world at:
http://streetpeeper.com

Visit this international magazine's website to discover more about music and fashion:
http://musicfashionmagazine.com

Read the online edition of leading British fashion and music title *Dazed & Confused* at:
www.dazeddigital.com

Note to parents and teachers
Every effort has been made by the Publisher to ensure that these websites contain no inappropriate or offensive material. However, because of the nature of the Internet, it is impossible to guarantee that the contents of these sites will not be altered. We strongly advise that Internet access is supervised by a responsible adult.

INDEX